Compassionate Estate Planning:
The Art of Eliminating Family Discord & Passing Values Forward

David Hudson, CEP®, RFC®

DEDICATION

This book is dedicated to my four grandsons: Preston, Jace, Ezra, and Joseph. They are four of my best friends. Their optimism, energy, and immeasurable faith in the future are a huge part of my inspiration to write. This book is written in hopes of leaving the world a better place for each of them.

CONTENTS

Acknowledgement   i

Preface   1

Introduction   3

1   Seize The Power   7

2   Promoting Peace & Love   25

3   What now?   33

4   Treasure   39

5   Troubled Waters   45

Appendix I   49

Appendix II   55

About the Author   61

ACKNOWLEDGEMENT

It has been said, "You can learn something from everyone." With that in mind, I would like to thank the many families I have worked with professionally over the years. Some have taught me the value of preparation by developing a plan and implementing it early in our professional relationship. It was a pleasure to watch their families when the plan was needed work in harmony without the fear of the unknown. I would also like to thank those that came seeking a plan, saw the need for a plan, and could afford to plan – but chose to procrastinate. As painful as the lesson was for their families when the plan was needed, I was vividly educated on the urgency of planning before the need arose. My heart broke for them, but the lesson wasn't wasted.

I would like to thank the group known as "the greatest generation." Men like my father, Preston Hudson, taught me the value of work. On days when the grind of running a business seemed too tiring, I could always look at his example and know that regardless of how weary you may be, you can always do the things you need to do. I learned from women like my mother, Nellie Hudson, the value of having empathy and compassion for others. She worked tirelessly to take care of her family and it never occurred to her to complain when things went wrong. I would also like to thank the thousands of individuals from that generation that passed forward to me the values and life lessons they learned throughout their lives. They have provided me with an education that is more valuable than gold and more priceless than rubies. It is the value of those lessons that have inspired me to write this book and share methods of passing them along to the generations that follow.

PREFACE

For twenty-seven years, I have had the privilege of interviewing senior citizens as part of my work; to me, they are a national treasure. I began in 1985 as an insurance agent and later, I earned the right to the titles Certified Estate Planner and Registered Financial Consultant. For years, I have had the privilege of helping seniors plan and, as an advisor, I have listened to their stories, absorbed their philosophies, and seen their wisdom. It has affected me and changed my life for the better.

As a member of the Baby Boomer generation, I have heard the expression "what a waste" used many times. Twenty-seven years ago when I first started dealing with senior citizens, I was dealing with people that were much different from today's seniors. In the early years, I dealt with individuals that had lived through the Great Depression and World War II. They didn't waste much. I gleaned great wisdom from them and I am indebted to them for the things they taught me. Many of them were what we call pack rats – they saved everything! One of their favorite sayings was, "You never can tell when you might need it."

Most of those great people have passed on now and on the other end of the spectrum are the young people of today. As a rule, they don't save anything – they truly are a throw-away generation. They grew up in a world where it was easier and less expensive to throw things away and buy new things. A problem arises for the younger generation when things becomes scarce, when the demand is much greater than the supply. What will happen to them when the supply is completely gone and the need is greater than ever? Though I could be talking about money and the national debt, I'm not. I refer to what will happen to the younger generation when the wisdom, values, and life lessons of the seniors and baby boomers are gone.

Over the years I have watched many from "the greatest generation" pass on. I am sad to report that each one that passed took part of their priceless wisdom and values with them. What if there were ways to preserve our values for future generations? What if there were ways to teach future generations the lessons we have learned through life experiences? What if we could help younger generations avoid making the mistakes we have made? What if we could reduce the chances that our families will be torn apart by selfishness after we are gone? In the pages of this book we will set forth ideas and methods that will help us accomplish these goals, so our values and life lessons are not wasted.

INTRODUCTION
SO, WHAT?

My college speech professor taught me so many important things about communicating ideas. Among the most important of his lessons was how important first impressions and first words can be. He taught that when you stand to speak, the first question you must immediately answer is, "So what?" In our modern world we are flooded with so much information that we must justify to our audience the value of our words. My name is _____, so what? I am from XYZ Company, so what? I have written a book, so what? Our world is filled with so many words and so much information that we must justify the value of the words we use. The answer to the "so what" question for this book is that it can improve the quality of your life and the lives of future generations if you apply the lessons taught herein.

The second major lesson I learned from my speech professor was the big difference in having to say something and having something to say. I have something to say. I have some very important things to say and I am excited about saying them to my readers.

Recently, a major insurance company did a survey concerning estate planning priorities. The survey was done throughout the United States and those surveyed were divided evenly between Baby Boomers and senior citizens. The survey found the list of priorities to be much different than most attorneys and financial planners would have thought they would have been.

The first priority on the list for the group was passing along "life lessons and values." Do you know any attorneys or financial planners that have methods in place to address this important priority? This is the number one priority among seniors and Baby Boomers, yet no one is addressing it. Do you know any attorneys or financial planners that know how to help you pass along your life lessons and values to future generations? Most likely you don't know one, but by the end of this short book you will.

The second most important issue to the group was knowing the instruction and wishes of their loved ones in times of crisis or end-of-life situations. According to a survey done by Lawyer.com in 2010, over 50% of the adult population does not have a properly prepared will. Dying without a properly prepared will could leave your family with major disadvantages. According to the same survey, 71% of those same adults do not have proper powers of attorney. If the percentages of individuals that do not have basic estate documents are that high, what do you think the odds are that loved ones are communicating with each other on the subject?

The third priority of those surveyed was passing on items of emotional value to their heirs. Most attorneys that have dealt with settling estates will tell you this is the biggest area of contention and family discord and this is the one area that seniors fear the most. They are wise enough to know it is a dangerous area that can divide families for generations to come, but they don't know how to fix the problem. By the end of this book you will know how to divide items that have great emotional value and also greatly reduce the chances of family discord.

The final priority on the list was the division of money and personal property. This is the area that attorneys and financial planners spend the most time on, yet it was only fourth on the list of priorities. In this book, we will deal with this area because it is very important. No one wants to work all of their life just to see the fruits of their labor taken away by taxes, legal fees, and government fees.

This book is intentionally short to make it easier and less time-consuming to read. It is written in a larger font than most books because it is for both the young and the old.

My hope is that it will aid families in discussing and planning for the future we will all eventually face. Once we have a plan for the more difficult times we can live free from worry about those times.

CHAPTER 1
SEIZE THE POWER

In the introduction, I mentioned a study that was recently done by a major life insurance company. The company surveyed over 2,700 individuals throughout the United States concerning estate-planning issues. The group was evenly divided between Baby Boomers born between 1946 and 1964 and senior citizens born before 1946. Those that responded to the survey agreed on their list of priorities for the issues. The number one priority was passing "values and life lessons" to the next generation. The second priority was having loved ones know wishes and instructions concerning crises and end-of-life situations. Third on the list was passing on property with emotional value to heirs without causing family discord. The fourth priority was passing money and assets to the next generation. Let's deal with these priorities in reverse order.

I place the money and property in the first chapter for two

important reasons. Out of honesty, I will tell you that I was afraid if I placed it in the fourth chapter many people would fail to read it and the information is very important. Secondly, it would be a mistake to believe money and property are the most important things in life, but it would be just as big of a mistake to think they are not important at all.

In my years of dealing with financial matters, I have had many people approach me about helping them with their planning. Many were almost apologetic. They normally would start the conversation by saying, "We know that we don't have much." The interesting part of that statement was that many of them were quite financially wealthy. How much they accumulated financially was just a matter of prospective.

I would normally explain to them my perspective on financial accumulation: Every person in this life did not start from the same place financially. Every person did not have the same educational opportunities, nor did they have the same business opportunities. As a general rule, my clientele worked hard for what they accumulated. Few were born into financial wealth and few inherited fortunes. If a person works for what they have, they spend time away from their family and loved ones. That is time they traded away that they could never buy back. Therefore, they traded away their most valuable asset (time) for the financial wealth they accumulated. On the last day of the individual's life, how much would they be willing to pay to have just a little of the time back? You may have heard that time is money. Many times that is true, but in a real sense, for most people, money is time. It represents time they have traded away for the money they have. To me, that makes managing their assets a sacred responsibility. To allow their assets to be wasted or taken away by the government needlessly is a crime I am not willing to commit. Therefore, if I know of a legitimate way to prevent it from happening, I will share that knowledge with my clients so they can do what they want with their hard-earned money. That's the reason a proper plan to pass on money and property to future generations is very important. Here are two important documents that you might consider using to pass property to your heirs.

Wills

Let me say once again, I am not an attorney and nothing I write should be construed to be personal legal advice. In this book, I will give some real examples of situations my clients have been through. Those examples are not meant to tell you what you should, or even could, do. They are examples that have taken place in the state I reside in and your state laws may be different. For that reason, you should educate yourself on the laws in your particular state and seek proper legal advice.

When most people think of a basic estate plan, they think of a will. A will is a legal document that expresses your wishes about several important matters. Normally a will tells the clerk of court or probate judge what your wishes are concerning the distribution of your personal property after your death. It also gives the court the name or names of the person or persons you want to be in charge of passing out your property to your heirs. If the person is a male, he is called an executor, and if the person is a female, she would be called an executrix. I believe the most important thing a will can do is name the person you choose to be guardian of your minor children if you have any.

A few months ago I had the opportunity to have lunch at school with my grandson. When his kindergarten teacher asked me about my profession, I told her I am a Certified Estate Planner and a Registered Financial Consultant. Her response was that she certainly did not need an estate planner. Many young people feel the same way. They believe that because they are young and have no intention of dying or becoming disabled, they do not need an estate plan and they certainly don't need a will. I would disagree with both of those assumptions.

Shortly after moving to my new hometown twenty-four years ago, a young friend had an auto accident. She was twenty-eight years old at the time. From the time she left the hospital until the day she died two years ago, she was in a nursing home. Do you think granting legal rights and letting loved ones know her wishes may have been important to her before the accident? After she had lost her ability to make decisions, it was too late. Does anyone remember the name, Terri Schiavo?

The main reason I believe a will is very important for young adults is because of the way children are treated under the law. Recently, I was at the home of a client and she was concerned about a young couple she knew. The couple had no will, but they had two young children. For some reason, they didn't want any of their relatives to become guardians of their minor children. Each parent had a $750,000 life insurance policy. That situation is a recipe for disaster for two important reasons.

Most importantly, if the couple dies they are leaving two children behind that are at the mercy of the legal system. The clerk of court or a judge would then have control of the immediate future of the children. Would the person making the decision controlling the future of the children have the same values and standards as their parents did? Would the person deciding the future of the children know the family history of relatives that may petition for guardianship? Why would good people that obviously love their children leave their future in the hands of someone they don't know, when making a will could fix the situation?

The second reason their situation is a recipe for disaster is because of the way money is handled for minors. An important question needed to be answered by this couple: Who would be the beneficiary of their life insurance?

Perhaps the couple had a friend in mind they would want to take care of the children. Did the couple leave $1.5 million dollars to a friend that would have no legal rights to the guardianship of the children, or were the children named as beneficiaries on the policies? What good would all of that money be to the children if the person that is getting it has no legal rights to be their guardian?

If the children are the beneficiaries of the money it can also be a disaster. In that case, the money would go into a trust account controlled by the state. Because of state statutes in my state, trust money is deposited into FDIC insured accounts. Those accounts are presently returning less than 1/10% per year. If the guardians (whoever that may be) need money for the children, they would have to ask for it from the court. The court has the power to grant the request or deny it. Even if the court has the best intentions for the money and the children, would the person controlling the money know the children and their needs? Would the person know the relatives that have guardianship of the children? Would the guardians be well-intentioned responsible adults or might they have taken the children to get access to $ 1.5 million dollars?

How could this situation be corrected? My recommendation would be that the couple talks to an attorney about the possibility of either setting up a trust, or doing a will with a minor's trust incorporated into it.

Can you see the dangers young couples with children face

in our legal system? The government official may be doing his or her best to help the children, however, no government official can know the needs of children the way loved ones can. If the problem is this large for couples, how much larger is it for single parents?

How serious should this problem be taken by grandparents? As a grandparent that has had the unpleasant experience of going to court to fight for visitation rights for two of my grandsons, I would not recommend you wait and hope it doesn't happen to you. While it is true that older adults need an estate plan, would you agree that perhaps the people that need a plan even more are people with minor children? A will is an important document for all adults regardless of age. You worked hard for the assets you have accumulated, why forfeit your rights to have a say in where it will go after you die?

Trust

There are many different types of trust with many different purposes. Irrevocable trust, special needs trust, and irrevocable life insurance trust can be used to accomplish great things in advanced estate planning. This book is not about advanced planning so I will not take time here to cover them. One more commonly used trust is the revocable living trust. One of the problems people have with a trust is that they don't know how they work or what they can accomplish. When the mere word trust is mentioned many people will stare into space with eyes glazed over. Many people believe a trust is so complicated that only geniuses and lawyers could possibly understand them. Many trusts can be complicated, but let's try to make it simple enough to understand without trying to cover the miniscule details.

Let's suppose you were in your attorney's office for a consultation one afternoon. After describing the goals you were trying to accomplish with your estate plan, your attorney recommends starting a revocable living trust. You think that sounds interesting and expensive, but you have no idea what a revocable living trust is, much less how it works. Your attorney walks over to his file cabinet and pulls out a box. On the side of the box he writes your name and the words revocable living trust. To you it looks like an ordinary box, but your attorney knows it is actually a magic box. It can do many things you can't do yourself. It can also do things that a will cannot do.

Magic sounds intriguing so you ask, "What magic things could the box possibly do for me?" Anthony, the attorney, slides a paper in front of you and at the top, in bold print, is printed, "Benefits of a Revocable Living Trust." You scan the list in your hand.

1. Assets in a Revocable Living Trust pass privately to your heirs after your death. Trust details are not public record like probate files are when

your property is passed on through a will. With a will anyone can see the details of your property and to whom it is given – with a trust they can't.

2. Money and property in a Revocable Living Trust does not pass through probate. This can save administrative costs and other fees.

3. Money and Property in a Revocable Living Trust can be given out slowly over a period of time that you choose. If you have heirs that are responsible with money they can receive their inheritance almost immediately. Your heirs that are poor money managers can receive their inheritance slowly over a period of years, if you choose. Your minor children don't have to receive all of their inheritance at age eighteen, when they reach the age of majority. Money and property can be given to them at predetermined ages that are chosen ahead of time by you.

4. Trust property (property owned by a trust) can avoid being frozen due to your death or disability.

5. A Revocable Living Trust will allow you to choose a manager(s) of your trust property if you become disabled, and will allow you to choose the person to manage, divide, and distribute your property after you die.

6. A Revocable Living Trust can contain moral clauses such a requirement to abstain from drug use or other damaging behavior.

7. A special type of Revocable Living Trust can allow married couples to have two estate tax exemptions.

After seeing the list of benefits, you are excited about a Revocable Living Trust and what it can do for you and your family. You tell your attorney to write one up for you. Anthony tells you that in order to draw up the trust, he needs three questions answered before you give him the details of what you would like to happen to your money and property.

First, Anthony needs to know who will put the assets in the trust once it's drawn up and properly signed. Of course, since it is your trust, you intend to put the money and property into the trust. He tells you that being the person that puts the property in your trust will give you a title, and that title is Grantor. Technically, that means you are the person making legal transfer, but in real life it means you are the person that will put the assets into the trust. He tells you that this is an important thing to do, because if the property isn't placed in the trust during your lifetime, the "trust magic box" will not keep it from going through probate.

Next he asked, "Who do you want to control your property?" You are a little taken aback by this question because you naturally assumed you could control your own property and money. You asked, "Can't I control my own money and property?" "Yes you can as long as you are alive and competent," he replies. "That would make you the Trustee of your trust." You now will be known as the Trustee (controller) of your trust property. You can do what you want to with the property as long as you are alive and competent. If you want to sell some property, you can sell it by signing as the Trustee. If you want to buy property and put it in your trust, you simply have the deed or title made in the name of your Trust and sign your name and title as Trustee. That sounds important. You have never been a trustee before. Now you are a trustee and a grantor.

Anthony asked his last of the three questions. "Whom do you want to benefit from the assets you are putting in your trust?" Of course, while you are alive, you want to benefit from the trust property. Benefiting from what's in your trust will make you the Beneficiary. So now you have found out that in a Revocable Living Trust you can be the Grantor (the person(s) that puts the assets in your trust), the Trustee (the person that controls the property in your trust), and the Beneficiary (the person that benefits from your trust).

The easy questions have been answered and now it is up to you to decide who will control your property when you are disabled or deceased. That person or persons will be your Successor Trustees. It is also up to you to decide who will get your property and when. Will you make provisions to have some of your assets distributed while you are still alive if you are disabled? When you die, who will receive the trust property, and when will they receive it? Do you have minors or others in mind that aren't good money managers? Do you need to distribute things to them over a predetermined period of time? Do you have children or other beneficiaries that have struggled with alcohol or drugs? Do they need to be monitored and have their inheritance given to them or withheld based on the results of the monitoring?

You look again at the list Anthony has given to you. At the moment you aren't completely sure of all of the answers to all of the questions you need to know about when and how each beneficiary will receive their inheritance. However, you are very sure that with a Revocable Living Trust you will have a lot of choices that you wouldn't have had with a will. At that moment, it occurs to you that there really isn't a magic box at all. Anthony was just using the box to help you understand how your trust could work and all the wonderful things it could do for you. When you put your property in the trust, it is like putting your property in the box. The lid on the box is open, so it symbolizes that you have complete access to the property to do with it whatever you want to. Finally anything in the box that could benefit you before can also benefit you now. The only thing missing from the box (your trust) is how you want your assets to be taken care of and when and how they will be given to others once you don't need them any longer.

This chapter has three important goals. It is very important for us to understand the importance of the money and property we accumulate during our lifetime. The things we worked so hard for and traded portions of our life for shouldn't be taken lightly. Most of us traded our time for the assets we have, and there is no more valuable commodity.

The second goal of the chapter is to familiarize each reader with the importance of having a will. It is important for everyone, but it is even more important for parents of minor children. Even those that choose to have a trust done will want a special type of will. If you don't bother to have one written for you, your state already has laws in place to control things for you and, more than likely, those laws will reflect the states values and wishes, not yours. By not having a will you are giving up a tremendous amount of control and most likely costing your heirs a lot of money, time, and heartaches.

The third goal of the chapter is to help each reader have some grasp of the benefits of a trust. While everyone doesn't need a trust, many problems can be solved by the use of a trust that can't be solved by a will.

This would be an excellent time for me to put in a disclaimer. I am not an attorney, and nothing I say or write should be construed to be legal advice. I am a trained Certified Estate Planner and a member of the National Institute of Certified Estate Planners. My training has prepared me with a general knowledge of all areas of estate planning. The training I have received has prepared me to help manage financial assets, work with attorneys as they prepare estate documents, and help with insurance matters. Though I will mention a few basic legal terms in this book, the book really is not about the legal side of estate planning. It is about the human side. It is not about the dry subject of estate documents. It deals with the areas of estate planning I am passionate about. The book deals with the love, respect, and control you have, and the ability to exercise both in the present and even beyond the grave.

A good attorney is necessary to have a complete estate plan. In my opinion, it is foolish to risk your assets and many of your family relationships trying to get "cheap" estate documents. If a person works all their life to accumulate the money and the property they own, why would that person even consider "do it yourself" documents? If that same person worked hard to build the relationships they have within their family, why would you risk division and discord by trying to put together a "cheap" estate plan? If the honest skilled mechanic that works on your car is worth every dime you pay him, and if the honest skilled surgeon that operates on you is worth the money he is paid, why would the honest skilled attorney not be worth his money too?

But how does one find an honest attorney? Due to the preconceived notions most of us have about lawyers, they are the easy targets for our jokes. It is easy to accept the stereotype that all attorneys are crooks. Though we know it isn't true, the thought is planted firmly in the backs of our minds. So how does one find a good lawyer? How does one find a good car dealer, a good financial planner, or a good mechanic? There are three important steps to finding a good car dealer, financial planner, or mechanic. The same three steps also apply to a good attorney.

First, one must get all the education that is reasonably available. Look for books at your local bookstore or library that will make complicated legal terms easier to understand. Browse the book to see if it is understandable before you take it home. I prefer books instead of the internet for most of my research. Unfortunately, anyone can post just about anything on the internet with or without proof of its validity Each year the American Bar Association publishes an excellent book on estate planning. A "Guide to Wills & Estates" is an excellent source of information for the layman. Regardless of your background, research is essential. It doesn't take many trips to the car lot to find that a well-educated consumer will get a better deal than a novice.

Secondly, after you have spent time educating yourself, question respected friends about the attorney they used for their documents. Don't be surprised if some of your most respected friends haven't done their estate planning yet either. Sometimes people that are otherwise very intelligent and educated procrastinate too. Ask the friends that have prepared about the way they were treated by the attorney that prepared their plan. Were they talked down to or treated with respect? Did they leave the attorney's office understanding what each document was designed to do for them personally? You should never ask the personal details of anyone's estate plan, but you do want to ask about how well the attorney explained things and how much respect he showed for each of your friends. If my friend volunteered the information about cost I would be appreciative for it, but I would not ask for the information.

Thirdly, you may want to shop around some. Attorneys are like any other businessperson. They are constantly seeking new clients. Many attorneys will offer a free consultation to prospective clients. Use this as an opportunity to gage your comfort level with the particular attorney. Don't be afraid or ashamed to ask about the cost of the services. Don't be afraid to ask for the quotes to be in writing. Remember that all lawyers are not created equally. If you need a simple will and powers of attorney, you may not want to pay for the services of an expensive estate-planning firm. On the other hand, if you have a more complicated estate that you believe may require one or more trust you probably don't want a "jack of all trades" lawyer handling it. I would look at any money spent as an investment that will pay big dividends in the future at a time when you or your family is most vulnerable. I have only two words of advice: first, do not be intimidated, and secondly, do not leave yourself and your family at the mercy of government officials by not having a proper plan.

This is the most technical and difficult of all the chapters to write and I'm sure it's also difficult to read. Because of the importance of the subject I made it chapter one. It is not the most important subject we will cover, but it would be an injustice if it were left out. Regardless of your choice my hope is that you will not choose to leave the power in the hands of the state. This is your time! Now, while you are alive and competent, you can make the choice to control the things you have given your life for! Seize the power!

CHAPTER 2
PROMOTING PEACE & LOVE

The biggest fear most clients face about dividing property is that the family will begin to quarrel and fight over the things that are left behind. In reality, many families split and never talk again over the settlement of an estate. It may surprise most people to know that the biggest arguments start over the smallest things. It isn't normally the house and land, nor is it the stocks, bonds, and bank accounts that cause the contention. Those items normally have a verifiable value. It doesn't take a genius to know that if you have a bank account with a value of $100,000 and each of the four children are to receive 25%; they will get $25,000 each. It's really hard to argue with those numbers. There may be a few people that will try, but they are the exception and not the rule.

Number three in the survey of concerns was passing items to the next generation with emotional value. There is good reason for this kind of anxiety. Many of the battles that turn into lifelong wars are over items that have little financial value – wars often start over things that have tremendous emotional significance. Things like grandmother's quilt, grandpa's shotgun, mom's china, or dad's fishing equipment can spark a fire that will turn into an endless inferno. While we all cringe at the thought of brothers and sisters not speaking to each other for years, we need to recognize the root of the problem in order to correct it. If the problem is a deep-seated resentment between family members that has existed for years, it is more difficult to correct than if it's a love and attachment to the person that is deceased. We will cover family resentment and contention in another chapter – in those cases it isn't really about the items. In this chapter, we will cover how to divide those things that have great emotional value without starting a war.

Emotional items are some people's way of feeling tied to someone that isn't with them any longer. These people feel the presence and love of a departed family member in the things they shared together while they were alive. The feelings are legitimate and the emotions are strong. There are two keys to helping family members continue to feel those strong emotions without causing a conflict.

The first key is to divide the items while you are still alive. If particular things represent an emotional bond and love the individual has for you, why not divide them while you are still alive to smooth over any misunderstandings? You don't have to give the articles away while you are still alive. You can, however, let each family member know that you are striving to give them the emotional satisfaction they will long for, even after you are gone.

The second key is to make sure each individual has a few things that will allow him or her to feel the connection they seek. With a little planning ahead, you can accomplish both goals. The time and effort taken to accomplish this goal will be time that will go a long way towards preserving family unity later.

It is important to start the conversation about what each individual wants as soon as it is reasonably possible. This will be a sensitive conversation and may not be easy. Expect to hear comments like, "I don't want to think about that," or, "You aren't going to die so I don't want to talk about it." Remember, you are asking someone that loves you to imagine life without you. If you choose to have the conversation in person, make sure to let them know you are talking to them as part of your estate planning process and not because you believe you will die soon. Begin by expressing your love for all the members of your family and tell them of your desire to keep love and unity in the family. Then ask the individual to thoughtfully write down eight to ten items they feel would be important to them. Ask each individual to write down a few lines about why each thing is important. Stress the need to have the completed list within seven to ten days.

Tell them they may not receive everything on their list, but you will try to make sure they get four or five items each.

In some cases, it may be impossible or unadvisable to talk person-to-person with your heirs. If that is the situation, it may be advisable to send each of them a letter. I suggest a letter because it is much more personal than an email or other correspondence. In the letter, you will want to incorporate the main ingredients of the above conversation. Let them know you are not writing because you believe you will become sick, disabled, or die soon. Explain that it is simply a part of planning your estate. Tell them your main motivation for planning is to promote the love and unity you want all of your heirs to have now and after you die. Stress the importance of listing items that each of them are attached to. Explain that you will do your best to fulfill their wishes, but please understand that you may only be able to fulfill a portion of them. If you choose to have a personal conversation, or use a letter, stress the importance of having each one reply within a week or ten days. If an heir procrastinates over ten days either verbally, or by letter, explain that you need the information promptly to complete your estate plan, and if you don't receive their list within a week, you will have to guess at what they would like to have. After the next week has passed, thoughtfully make the list for them. With each important object write a brief explanation of why you believe it is important to them. There is no better way to cause discord than to let one procrastinator block the wishes of all the others.

When you receive all the lists from each loved one, read each list carefully and try to weigh the emotional strength of each request. You may want to try your best to make sure each heir receives at least half of the articles on their list. Remember, the strength of the emotional pull is much more important than the number of things each one will receive. If your daughter made Christmas cookies with you and her grandmother, a rolling pin and cookie cutters may hold tremendous value to her. If two heirs want the same things, you may have some tough decisions to make and you may need to ask yourself some tough questions. Overall, which one is getting the items that have the most sentimental value to them? How powerful are the emotional attachments each one has for this particular object? Which of them is most likely to be upset by not receiving it? Could one be happy with a substitute? Making these decisions may not be easy, but making them while you are alive can give you the opportunity to smooth over any hard feelings and avoid a family split later. One word of warning here is appropriate: please do not procrastinate once you have the information you asked for. If you know their wishes and you choose to ignore them, it could only make matters worse.

Now that you have their lists, what will you do with them? One possibility is to gift the items to each heir while you are still living. If you choose to make gifts, there are several important things to remember. First, in order to maintain unity, you need to record on paper the items you are giving away and to whom they are being given to. Make sure to sign each paper – and having each one notarized isn't a bad idea.

There are limits to how much you can give away to each person without filing gift tax forms. At the time of the writing of this book, if an individual gives more than $13,000 to another individual in any year, the giver is required to fill out a gift tax form. Unless the gift is huge, there will be no gift tax due, but the forms still need to be filled out.

In order for an article to be gifted legally, it must be given "with no strings attached." That means you cannot put any restrictions on what the receiver does with the gift after you have given it to them. If you retain any rights or control over the gift, it is not technically a gift. This is an important consideration when dealing with your future heirs. If the person isn't very responsible; if they have judgments and lean against them; or if they are in a marriage that may break up, be very careful. You may want to use another method of getting property to them.

The final important fact about gifts is that they may be stored any place the receiver wants them to be stored. For example, if you wanted to gift your grandmother's bedroom suit to your daughter and she chose to store the bedroom suit in your extra bedroom where it is now it is still a gift. However, it is imperative that she chooses to do it of her own free will. If your shotgun is in the bedroom closet and you gift it to your grandson, your grandson may choose to store it in the closet where it is now. As long as he decides where it is stored, it is still a gift. However, if he later chooses to take the shotgun to his house, it is his right to take it.

Another method of passing property to your heirs is to have the instructions written into your will or trust. When dealing with minor children or heirs that have financial problems, you need to remember that property passed through a will is given to each adult individual as soon as the probate process is completed, and property given to minors will be given at the time each child reaches the age of majority. Property passed to heirs through a trust can be given immediately to adults, be held in trust for the benefit of minors, or be given to individuals over a set period of time that you have chosen.

In order to incorporate your list into your will or trust, it is best to have the information amended into your will or trust. I highly recommend you have an attorney do it for you. The amendment shouldn't be very expensive and it will be a great investment toward promoting family unity for years to come.

If you are having new estate documents written it may be

possible to have your attorney insert a sentence or paragraph into your will or trust that allows you to leave handwritten instructions with the document. The sentence could say something like, "In the event I have left handwritten instruction with (this will, or this trust) I direct that those instructions be followed as closely as if they were a part of this document." Such a sentence in a legal document may or may not be legal in your state. It certainly would be worth asking your attorney to find out.

In order to give those you love the best chance of avoiding conflicts and hard feelings, it is vital that you take the steps necessary to deal with this emotionally charged area of estate planning. It has been my experience, that even in the best families small things can cause huge problems. Families that have never experienced conflict can find division and strife boiling over in the middle of the settling of an estate. Many times the parent or loved one that is no longer there was the glue that held the family together. For that reason, it is critical for the sake of the family that conflicts are settled before that person is gone. Please don't procrastinate.

CHAPTER 3
WHAT NOW?

From our survey, we found the second most important issue to baby boomers and senior citizens is to have their loved ones know their wishes in times of crisis. Many families that face major decisions after a crisis find themselves asking the question, "What now?" This priority presupposes two important facts. The first fact is that there can be times of crisis in the lives of those we love. Many younger people refuse to accept that fact or even think about it. When you begin planning you may hear comments like, "We're not going to talk about that because it isn't going to happen to you." Many children act as if nothing bad will ever happen if they refuse to talk about it or plan for it. To those sons and daughters, you should ask if they would also feel better if you took the spare tire out of your car. If nothing bad will happen because you refuse to prepare, removing the spare tire will guarantee you will never have a flat tire on a dark road, right? If your children or heirs are like that, you may have to be firm and explain that you are planning for events you hope will never happen. However, having plans and not needing them is far superior to needing plans and not having them.

The other presupposition is that it is possible to let those you love know what you want to happen ahead of time. This is a very important point, because many people will be unable to communicate with their loved ones at some point in the future. Some will be diagnosed with Alzheimer's or Dementia, others may have stokes, and some will be in accidents and no longer have the ability to communicate. To presuppose that it is possible to communicate your wishes concerning what you would want to happen in times of crisis is wise. To presuppose that you will always be able to communicate as well as you do now would be very unwise. This fact highlights the need to plan now, rather than later.

One situation that we need to plan for is the possibility of becoming disabled. If you are a baby boomer or a senior citizen, you have lived long enough to know that being prepared for a crisis has no effect on whether the crisis will happen or not. You also know that sometimes bad things happen to good people.

There are at least three important legal documents that you need to investigate when dealing with your healthcare. By having these documents prepared ahead of time, you can save your loved ones a multitude of headaches and money. These are important documents and while having them prepared is very important, it is also important to go a step farther and communicate your wishes to those that will be responsible if you are unable to communicate.

Durable Power of Attorney

A Durable Power of Attorney is a document that allows another person (your agent) to conduct business on your behalf. It is durable because it allows your agent to conduct business for you even when you are disabled. The power of attorney can allow your agent to write checks on your bank account to pay bills. It can allow that person to file income and property tax for you. A well-drawn Durable Power of Attorney can allow your agent to invest your assets. It can also give your agent the ability to provide support for your loved ones using your financial resources.

A word of caution is in order at this point: the Durable Power of Attorney is only as safe and reliable as the person you appoint as your agent. If the person you appointed is dishonest or unreliable, any property you give them authority over may be at risk.

If you aren't sure you have anyone that you can trust with that much responsibility, you might want to use joint agents or professionals to look after your business. One other suggestion you may want to discuss with your attorney is the possibility of making it a "spring power of attorney" that only goes into effect when you become disabled.

It is important that you are comfortable with whomever you chose, and that the person or persons know where your assets are. They also need to know what your financial goals are and who trusted advisors are.

Healthcare Power of Attorney

Your Healthcare Power of Attorney will allow a person you choose to make healthcare decisions for you. This could be the same or different person as the one you appoint as your agent to handle your business in your Durable Power of Attorney. If you are blessed to have a trustworthy person that is honest and great with money, you may want to use them as your agent to handle your business. If you have a person that is knowledgeable with healthcare issues, you may want them to be your healthcare agent. Those two responsibilities could be handled by the same person or by different people. Two or more individuals could handle the responsibilities jointly, but they would need to be in agreement.

Whomever you choose to be your agent for your

Healthcare and Durable Powers of Attorney, two factors
are vitally important if you choose to use different
individuals to hold these important positions. Both agents
need to be able to work well together and each individual
will need to have a clear understanding of what and how
you want things to happen. If you become incapacitated,
do you want to stay at home or go into a nursing home?
Are your wishes practical? What financial arrangements
have you made to cover the cost? Will assets need to be
liquidated? If so, in what order should they be liquidated?
The best time to have this conversation is when you
originally form your estate plan. Each time you update
your plan, be sure to review your wishes with those you
are depending on to make decision for you.

The Alternative

In most cases having proper powers of attorney is much
better than the alternative. You could refuse to legally
designate the person(s) to be responsible for making your
decisions in the event you become disabled. If you decide
not to designate anyone, your state has a procedure to
make choices for you. In many states, the process is called
guardianship.

With no plan in place the state could be forced to hold a
competency hearing. At the competency hearing, the state
could appoint a guardian over you and your affairs. Your

guardian may be your closest relative or it may be a total stranger. If you are fortunate enough to have a close relative appointed as your guardian, that person may have to ask the court for permission to make any changes to your finances or healthcare. Each month your guardian could be required to give financial reports to the court, and each year the guardian could be required to give an annual accounting, detailing all financial transactions. Of course, fees and expenses would accompany each accounting. More often than not, the court will require your guardian to pay for an expense bond to assure they act solely on your behalf.

Laws may vary from state to state, but guardianship is seldom a wise or pleasant choice. My clients that have experienced it compared it to their worst nightmares. If you have a tendency to procrastinate or to leave important tasks undone, you may want to investigate what the process is in your state for dealing with assets and healthcare decisions for people that fail to plan.

CHAPTER 4
TREASURE

Most of us have a loved one or a friend that has helped mold our lives. There is no doubt that if that person has passed on, you miss them very much. You may remember their words, their mannerisms, and their deeds. The more you have to remember the person by, the closer you may feel to them. The person may live on through you in the values and life lessons you learned from them. Unfortunately, the more time that passes, the less clear your memories may be. Most of the priceless memories we have of loved ones are of events we didn't plan. Things just happened that we remember, and we carry those memories with us. Regrettably, as time passes we remember those important events less vividly.

In the past, little has been done to preserve the values and life lessons of the "average" person. I am hopeful that this will change soon. Think of the person you love most that has already passed away? Do you remember their voice and mannerisms? Do you remember their stories and their laugh? Until now, those priceless treasures have rarely been preserved.

I have done retirement planning for hundreds of clients over the years. The things they have accumulated are important and the objects that bring back their memories to us are of the utmost importance. However, the values they have taught us and the lessons we have learned from those we love most are priceless treasures that we have done little to protect. That is a mistake I would like to eliminate.

Do a little exercise with me. Close your eyes and think of your closest family member or loved one that has passed away. Imagine if that person could spend the next hour with you. What would you say to them? What would you like to have them say to you? If you could have one more hour with that person, how valuable would it be to you? Do you think you would want to record the conversation?

Now think of the person you love most that is still alive. Are you completely sure of how long they will live? Is it possible that one day you will long to hear their voice the way you long to hear the voice of your loved one that is already gone? Is there anything you could do now to make sure that when that day comes, you will have living memories of them?

Have you ever thought about interviewing the person and recording their answers? At this time in history, the possibilities are almost limitless. Could you ask questions and make notes of your loved one's answers? Could you write their stories as they tell them to you? Could you buy an inexpensive audio recorder and record the conversation? Could you set up a video recorder on a tripod and record the interview to be seen later, even after the person is gone? If you wanted to get more elaborate, could you hire a videographer to record and edit the interview with your loved one?

Now think back once more to the exercise we were doing? Remember the loved one that is already gone? What would a recorded conversation with that person be worth to you today? If you had a recording that reflected that person's life lessons and values would you be richer for it? Could that recording enrich the lives of generations to come? Obviously, you can't go back in time and record the voice of someone that has already passed away, but could you record your own message or the message of your loved ones that are still here?

If you were interviewing someone, what would you ask him or her? Naturally you can ask anything you would like to. You can make up your own questions. You could think of the special memories you share with the person and record them for future generations. You could ask them about life lessons they have learned and how they learned them. You could record stories they have told in the past. You could record a message to each child or grandchild. Again, the possibilities are limitless.

Many people aren't sure how to start the conversation about making values and life lessons a part of a complete estate plan. Does recording the memories we would like to share need to be a major undertaking? Why couldn't it be as simple as asking a question or a series of questions? Why couldn't it be as simple as saying, "Mom or Dad, you know how much the lessons I have learned from you mean to me. Would you mind if I asked you some questions and we record the answers?" You could say, "Grandmother or Grandfather, you know how much I love your stories. Would you mind if I record you while you told some of them?" You could even say, "I have some questions that are important to me, would you mind if I asked them and we record your answers?"

Of course, it would also be wise to record a message for those you love. As part of a complete estate plan, everyone should record the values and lessons they would like to pass on. Whether you are recording a personal legacy message or one for someone else, make sure to keep a few important thoughts in mind.

First, try to make your message brief. From the beginning to the end, it shouldn't be any more than one hour. The exception may be when you are recording a message for each child or each grandchild – the message to each one should still be brief, but the total length of all of your messages doesn't have to be less than an hour.

Second, use the highest quality tapes, CDs, or DVDs you

can find. You will want this to be a legacy that will last for years to come. What could be worse than making the recording, then years later, when someone you love wants to hear your message, they find a blank recording?

Third, try to organize your thoughts. Don't ramble! If you are recording your own message for the future you may want to write the message out first. Once you begin recording, DO NOT read the messages you have written out. Use your written message to organize your thoughts and as an outline to keep you on track. Speak from your heart; speak naturally.

Finally, try to make the experience as positive as possible. Ask positive questions that will have positive responses. This is not the time to bring up bad memories or bad experiences from the past. There may be one exception to that rule, yet I'm not sure if it is even totally negative. Remember, in a heart-to-heart message with children, grandchildren, or heirs, this could be a good time to share your thoughts and admonish them not to have discord. There is probably no time when their hearts will be more tender than when they hear your message after you have gone. Even if you choose this time to do that, I still would not bring up a lot of negative history in the process.

Still not sure what to say in a message? Don't worry! Below I have a list of what I call "memory joggers" that may be helpful for you. They are short questions or phrases that have been useful in getting a person to think about what to say. Your list may be better than mine, but perhaps my memory joggers will be useful to some of you.

Memory Jogger #1 Is there a special story or life lesson that you would like to pass on to those you love?

Memory Jogger #2 Are you passing along some possession that has special sentimental value to each of your love ones. Have you thought of recording what the item is and the memory behind why it is so special?

Memory Jogger #3 Are there some instructions you would like to leave to each individual loved one, your spouse, your executor, or your trustee?

Memory Jogger #4 Are there some final instructions you would like to leave to each individual loved one, your spouse, your executor, or your trustee? This may be a good time to admonish everyone to get along with each other.

Memory Jogger #5 – Think of the person you love the most that has passed away. What message, thoughts, or story would you like to have had them record for you? Would you like to record a similar thought for those you love?

CHAPTER 5
TROUBLED WATERS

Hopefully by now we know that an estate plan is not just a group of documents drawn by an attorney, though we know how important those documents are. Now we know a complete estate plan is much more. We know how important it is to family unity to have a plan in place to give out those items with emotional value. We know how important it is to have our loved ones know what to do in emergency situations both before and after we are gone. We know the crown jewel of our estate plan is the recorded messages we leave to those we love most. Those messages will help them remember our stories, values, and life lessons. With such a complete estate plan there should be no room for any problems, right?

The answer is maybe and maybe not. For most people, such a complete estate plan will greatly reduce the chances of conflict. However, no plan can guarantee there will be no conflict. When a loved one dies, it is an emotionally-charged time. In many families, there are strong feelings and strong personalities. Many families have one child that has a dominant personality. There are times when it isn't the son or daughter that is dominate, but a son-in-law or daughter-in-law. This can be positive or it can be negative.

I recently dealt with a family of five children. The mother had been one of my clients for years. She had passed away a short time earlier. One of the daughters had a strong personality and everyone knew she was well educated and fair – no one resented her. The fact that she had a strong personality did not bother any of her siblings. To them, it was a blessing to have her look after their mother's estate. The family worked as well together as any I have had the privilege of dealing with. I wish every family had the same relationships and bonds as that group did – obviously some don't. Groups like them are a pleasure to deal with and if you are blessed with such a family you have a lot to be thankful for.

Many times a family will have unresolved issues that have been brewing for years. Perhaps a brother or sister isn't perceived as being fair and open. The perception may or may not be correct and it may come from a single incident that happened years ago or it may come from a lifetime of conflict. Broken relationships can be very complicated. It would be very presumptuous of me to think that I could give advice here about how to repair such relationships.

However, there are a few things I can tell you about

broken relationships from experience. First, your best chance of repairing the break may be sooner rather than later. Perhaps you could speak to the parties at first separately and then together in hopes of making peace. Second, if they both love you, their hearts will never be more tender than they will after you have just passed away. Have you thought about asking them to reunite in your "values and life lessons" message to them? Finally, and unfortunately, there are some broken relationships that will never be repaired. While it is certainly worth the effort to most people to regain family unity, we won't always be successful; and though we won't always be successful we can all try our best. When we have done that much, we have to be at peace with the results.

It is my hope that this book has given you a greater understanding of estate planning and how important it is. I hope you not only know now how important it is for everyone, but how important it is to you personally. My hope is that you no longer see estate planning as a stack of dry complicated legal documents that you would prefer not to think about, but as a magical process that can extend your values and influence many years after you are gone. More than anything, my hope is that you and those you love most will be richer because you chose to act on what you have found in the pages of this book.

APPENDIX I
THE ICEBURG

You are retiring soon. You have planned well. You have changed your financial planning strategy from the accumulation phase to the distribution phase. You have finished this book and you have completed your estate plan. You are feeling great about your planning strategy. You feel safe and secure, like you have all the bases covered.

You have done a great job, one that far exceeds the job most of your peers do. You are to be congratulated. However you are missing one small hazard that could become the iceberg that sinks your retirement Titanic. No book on estate planning would be complete without addressing long-term sickness and disability.

According to the National Clearing House for Long Term Care Information, at age 65, one in three retirees will need some type of care for ninety days or longer. As you get older, your chances increase significantly. If you are female, the odds are almost twice as high of needing care as they are for a male. Living alone can also increase your chances of needing care.

For our purposes, I will define long-term care as any care required by a person for a period of ninety days or more due to a sickness or accident. The care could be given in the home by home health care professionals, at an adult daycare center, at an assisted living facility, or at a nursing home. Regardless of what type of care a person needs, it can be very expensive.

According to the Genworth Financial's 2012 Cost of Care Survey, the national average cost of a semi-private bed in a nursing home is $72,000 per year. The same survey found a single bedroom in an assisted living facility is $39,600 annually. For eight hours per day of home health care, five days per week, the average cost was $39,520 per year, while five days per week of adult day care would cost about $15,860 each year.

As you can see, long-term care costs could knock a sizable hole in your retirement plans. So what plans could you make to cover such cost? There are four basic trains of thought on the matter.

Self-Insuring

Many people choose to self-insure and take the chance that they will not be the one in three that need care. If you are among these risk takers, I hope you have deep pockets and hopefully you won't need care anytime soon. If you retire today at age 65, it could easily be fifteen years before you need the long-term care. By that time, the semiprivate nursing home room that cost $72,000 today will cost $184,320 per year based on a five percent compound inflation rate.

Long-Term Care Insurance

Many seniors have chosen to share the risk with insurance companies by taking out long-term care insurance. There are some excellent companies available that offer outstanding products. The advice I offer many of my clients about long-term care insurance is to buy the amount you need. You have a one in three chance you will need long-term care for ninety days or longer. That is a substantial risk considering you have a one in fifteen hundred chance your house will burn down. If you insure your house, it is logical to insure your need for a long-term stay in a nursing home. On the other hand, it also means you have a two in three chance you will not need long-term care. Like most health insurance policies, if you never use the benefits the insurance company will keep the money when you die or drop your coverage. If the average nursing home in your area charges $72,000 per year for a bed, and you have income of $24,000 per year, could it make sense to only insure the $48,000 per year difference and save 33% on your premiums? ($72,000 nursing home cost - $24,000 of income = $48,000 needed to pay the bill). This may not fit your specific situation but it is worth some thought.

Asset-Based Long-Term Care Insurance

Many of my clients have found asset-based long-term care to be an excellent way to protect their retirement from the financial devastation a long-term care stay can cause. Over the last five years, many people have found they have money making very little returns. If the money is in a certificate of deposit, the interest they are paid is taxable. They find their money isn't working very hard for them. For some clients the thought of purchasing traditional long-term care insurance is not very appealing. If they are older, the prices are very high. If they are younger, they may have to pay premiums for many years before they use the coverage. The answer for these people may be an asset-based long-term care policy. The way it works is simple: the client transfers funds from an investment and the funds are put on deposit with an insurance company – in the form of an annuity or a life insurance policy. They can expect to receive little or no returns on their new policy, but if they need long-term care, their policy will pay all of their money back to them and continue to pay the long-term care bills for a substantial time, even after all of their money is gone. If the person never needs the long-term care, the amount of money they deposited or almost all of the money they deposited would be returned to their heirs. Many of my clients believe if they need the coverage for long-term care, they are winners; yet if they never need the long term care, they avoided losing. This description is not meant to be a full disclosure or a recommendation for any individual, but a general description of how asset-based long-term care insurance can work.

Relying of Government Benefits

There are several different kinds of government benefits that seniors feel like they could rely on if they needed to go into a nursing home. I will address three of them here.

Medicare has very limited benefits for nursing homes or home health care. They may pay for some rehabilitation after a hospital stay, but any other care must be in the skilled care unit. The maximum amount of time Medicare will pay a nursing home is one hundred days. Remember our definition of long-term care? Our definition was "any care required by a person for a period of ninety days or more due to a sickness or accident." It has been my experience that getting Medicare to pay for ninety days or more is slim to none.

Veterans Administration benefits are provided for veterans and there may be some benefits for the wives of veterans. At the writing of this book, many veterans and/or their spouses are receiving a benefit called "Aid and Attendance." It is a benefit I believe is well deserved. The full benefit is not enough to pay the average price of a nursing home or assisted living facility, but it can certainly help. There are other benefits available for those with service-related disabilities. I would recommend you contact your local chapter of the Disabled American Veterans for more information and help – you deserve any help you can get.

Medicaid is the government program that was started in 1965 to help the indigent. Medicaid is paid for by both state and federal funds and the rules for receiving benefits vary from state to state – I will not address the specifics here. I will say that at one time, Medicaid was much easier to qualify for than it is now. Over the years, the federal and state governments have faced shortfalls. As government money has gotten more scarce over the years, the rules for receiving benefits have gotten more and more stringent. In my state, a single nursing home resident is limited to owning $2,000 in assets and receiving thirty dollars a month in income. There are a few small exceptions for a burial life insurance policy and a prepaid burial plan, but the requirements are very strict.

APPENDIX II
THE LIFE SAVER

For many years now, I have had access to a great product that has gotten a very bad reputation for a lot of good reasons. One of the main reasons is the people that have marketed the product and their tactics in selling it.

Many people feel life insurance is a horrible waste of money. After interviewing clients for well over twenty-five years, I understand why so many of them feel that way. Many have purchased it from a salesperson that was more interested in the size of their commission check than in the needs of their clients. Others have bought the wrong kind of insurance. In the large majority of cases, the buyer has bought a policy with no clue as to why they bought the particular death benefit they did. I would estimate that ninety-five percent of the times I have asked a prospective client why they have a particular amount of insurance they have no clue why they bought the amount. Isn't it strange how many people from so many different backgrounds have $50,000, $100,000, or $250,000 life policies? If I asked them why they have a particular kind of life insurance they don't know that either. How sad is it that a product that has the potential to do so much good is so misunderstood because of the people that are peddling it?

I believe there are two vital rules to purchasing life insurance. Rule one is to purchase only the amount you will need in the future – do not over or under buy. Since the future is unknown, you should have particular needs in mind. For example, a young married couple that has plans to start a family soon may need a large amount of life insurance to cover the needs of the family they plan to start. A senior citizen that needs a burial insurance policy may only need a small death benefit, while a high net worth couple that is planning their estate may need a specific amount to cover their estate tax. It is very important that each individual knows the purpose for the amount of coverage he or she is carrying.

The second rule is to purchase the kind of life insurance you need. In order for the young couple to get the amount they need and keep it affordable, they will likely need to purchase term insurance. If they need more permanent insurance later, the term insurance will assure them they can purchase it even if they develop health problems. The older person that is looking for a policy to cover final expenses will need a whole life policy; and the high net worth couple will more than likely want a survivorship life policy to provide the money for estate tax when the last spouse dies.

Let me take a moment to discuss determining the correct amount of coverage. It should be relatively simple to determine the amount a funeral will cost in a number of years for the senior that wants to cover those expenses. On the other hand, the amount that would be needed to pay estate tax could be a very complicated process requiring the input of the couple's financial advisor, CPA, and attorney. For the young couple to determine the specific amount they need, it would require that a needs analysis should be completed. The amount that would be required to cover the needs of a young family if they lost their main source of income would be huge. Many young people can't imagine carrying a life insurance policy that large. Let me use this young couple to illustrate the miracle of a product that is so misunderstood.

Let's suppose that Joe is the twenty-eight year old father of two young children. His son, Bob, is three and his daughter, Grace, is five. His friend, Jim, is a life insurance agent. After doing the needs analysis with Joe, Jim determines that he needs a life insurance policy with a $750,000 death benefit. Joe is stunned by the amount Jim is suggesting he purchase. He feels the agent is inflating the amount to make a high commission. He is offended and he objects forcefully. Jim being older and wiser understands his reaction. Jim says, "Joe if I gave you a briefcase with $750,000 in it, that would be a lot of money wouldn't it?" Joe acknowledges that it would be a huge amount of money. "Joe," the agent says, "what if I told you, you could have the money under one condition?" "What condition?" Joe asked. "The condition is that you would never be able to earn another dollar for the rest of your life. That money has to last you and your family for as long as you live. You will need to send your children to college with it. You can have the money but you can never earn another dollar. Is that still a great deal for you?" Joe thinks of all the bills he and his family will face over their lifetime. He thinks about his son and daughter in high school and in college. He thinks of their family vacations and about his little girl's wedding day. Joe realizes it really isn't such a huge amount after all. To accept what seems like such a huge amount of money with no way to earn more isn't great at all! The agent looks into his friend's eyes and simply says, "If you take out this policy and you die, that is exactly what you are asking your family to do. When you stop breathing you will never be able to earn another dollar to take care of their needs. In our analysis I asked the questions and you gave me the numbers. They aren't my numbers they are yours. If you want me to quote a much smaller amount I can do that for you, but I would prefer to quote the amount you said your family would need."

I use that illustration to make a simple point that escapes many people. There is only one reason to carry life insurance. Life insurance is always bought and paid for in order to make the lives of those left behind easier. Life insurance, in so many ways, is a financial miracle of love. It is food on the table, it is the mortgage payment to keep the roof over the heads of those you love, it is the heat they will need to stay warm in the winter, it is the gifts under the tree every Christmas when you are no longer with them.

In 2002, my oldest son joined a special, select group that not just anyone can join. They are somewhat like a family and they don't all know each other, but they all have taken the same oath. They will sacrifice for each other when it is required. The oath requires them to make sure they leave no one behind and if one falls in battle the others will make sure he isn't left behind. You may have guessed that I am talking about the United States Marine Corp.

Please don't misunderstand my illustration. I love and respect our military, especially the Marines, and I hold them in the highest regard. Many years ago when my children were small, I joined a special group when I purchased a life insurance policy. It was an inexpensive term life policy and it didn't build any cash value. I didn't know all the people in the group, but the group also had some requirements to join. We made a pledge to each other and that pledge was that if one of us were to die, the rest of us would sacrifice by paying premiums to make sure that person's family had the money they needed to live. I paid my premiums and never collected a dime from the policy I paid for. That was a sacrifice that I gladly made. Someone's family that joined that group no doubt did collect. That is the way life insurance works. We all hope we won't be the one to collect, however, we know that if we need it, those we love will be taken care of even when we aren't there. The miracle of life insurance is that we can all sacrifice a little to provide for those we love in case we aren't there for them. For pennies while we are here, we can provide dollars for those we love most when we aren't.

There are many great opportunities available to diligent investors that are willing to educate themselves today. However, there is no financial vehicle available now, or at any time in the past, that can accomplish what life insurance can accomplish. When a qualified insurance professional takes the time to determine the proper amount of coverage to meet the specific need of a client and recommends the appropriate plan of coverage, there is no product in the history of the world that can match what life insurance can do for those you love most.

ABOUT THE AUTHOR

David Hudson is the founder and president of Master's Estate and Financial Services in Hickory, NC. In 2012, he founded Hudson Estate and Financial Consulting LLC. He has served those that have retired and those that are soon to retire in the Catawba Valley Area of North Carolina for over twenty-seven years. His greatest asset during that period has been his ability to listen and learn from the clients he serves. In 2001, David completed requirements and was awarded the designation of Certified Estate Planner by the National Institute of Certified Estate Planners. In 2005, the International Association of Registered Financial Consultants awarded him the designation of Registered Financial Consultant. Now his burning desire is to bridge the chasm between the "greatest generation" and the generations that follow.

17131219R00039